Community Helpers

Couriers

by Terri DeGezelle

Consultant:
Bob DeCaprio
Executive Director
Messenger Courier Association of the Americas

Bridgestone Books
an imprint of Capstone Press
Mankato, Minnesota

Bridgestone Books are published by Capstone Press
151 Good Counsel Drive, P.O. Box 669, Mankato, Minnesota 56002
http://www.capstone-press.com

Library of Congress Cataloging-in-Publication Data
DeGezelle, Terri, 1955–
    Couriers/by Terri DeGezelle.
    p. cm.—(Community helpers)
    Includes bibliographical references and index.
    ISBN 0-7368-0957-0
    1. Express service—Juvenile literature. 2. Messengers—Juvenile literature. I. Title.
II. Community helpers (Mankato, Minn.)
HE5881 .D43 2002
651.3'743—dc21   00-012543

Summary: A simple introduction to the work couriers do, the tools they use, the people
    who help them, and their importance to the communities they serve.

Editorial Credits
Sarah Lynn Schuette, editor; Karen Risch, product planning editor; Linda Clavel,
    cover designer; Heidi Schoof, photo researcher

Photo Credits
Capstone Press/Gary Sundermeyer, 4, 6, 10, 18
David F. Clobes, Stock Photography, 8, 12
International Stock/Vli Degwert, cover
Photo Network/Mark Sherman, 16; Al Cook, 20
Photri-Microstock, 14

**Bridgestone Books thanks Willmar C. Schuette for providing props for photographs
    in this book.**

1 2 3 4 5 6 07 06 05 04 03 02

Table of Contents

Couriers 5

What Couriers Do 7

What Couriers Drive 9

Where Couriers Work 11

Tools Couriers Use 13

What Couriers Wear 15

Skills Couriers Need 17

People Who Help Couriers 19

How Couriers Help Others 21

Hands On: Address and Deliver a Letter 22

Words to Know 23

Read More 24

Internet Sites 24

Index 24

Couriers

Couriers deliver letters and packages to homes and businesses. They work in small towns and large cities. People depend on couriers to deliver items on time.

deliver
to take or to bring
something to someone

What Couriers Do

Couriers pick up packages and letters from warehouses. The packages sometimes hold computers, toys, or books. Couriers pick up important papers and letters from offices. They then deliver the items to the correct address.

What Couriers Drive

Many couriers drive delivery trucks to transport packages and letters. They also drive vans and cars. Some couriers even ride bikes. Courier companies use airplanes, ships, and trains to transport packages and letters.

transport

to move or to carry something from one place to another

9

Where Couriers Work

Couriers work for small and large companies in many towns and cities. Some couriers travel around the world to deliver packages and letters.

Tools Couriers Use

Couriers use maps to find driving directions. They need to plan the best route to make fast deliveries. They use computers to keep track of packages. Couriers use scanners to read addresses printed on packages and letters.

route
the road or course people follow to get from one place to another

13

What Couriers Wear

Couriers wear uniforms. These uniforms can be many colors such as brown, blue, white, or green. Couriers who walk long distances wear comfortable shoes. Many couriers also wear name tags.

Skills Couriers Need

Couriers need to deliver letters and packages on time. They need to be able to follow directions and read maps correctly. Couriers should be friendly and polite to customers.

customer
a person who buys goods or services

People Who Help Couriers

Many people work together to deliver packages and letters quickly. Sorters help couriers weigh and sort the items people want to send. Dispatchers tell some couriers where to pick up packages.

dispatcher
a person who gives
messages or directions

19

How Couriers Help Others

Couriers deliver items that customers order from catalogs. They also deliver medicine to hospitals. They bring gifts to children. Couriers deliver important packages to people around the world.

catalog
a book with a list of items that people can order from a company

21

Hands On: Address and Deliver a Letter

Couriers deliver packages and letters. In this activity, you will learn how to address a letter correctly and then deliver it.

What You Need

Piece of paper
Pen or pencil
Envelope
Phone book
An adult

Your Name
Street Address
City, State, Zip Code

Name
Street Address
City, State, Zip Code

What You Do

1. Write a letter to a neighbor.
2. Fold the letter, put it in an envelope, and seal the envelope.
3. Ask an adult to help you look up your neighbor's address.
4. Follow the diagram above and write the address in the middle of the envelope.
5. Next, write your address in the upper left corner of the envelope. This is your return address.
6. Deliver the letter to the person. Ask an adult to go with you.

Words to Know

customer (KUHSS-tuh-mur)—a person who buys goods or services; couriers deliver items to customers.

dispatcher (diss-PACH-ur)—a person who gives messages or directions to some couriers

scanner (SKAN-uhr)—a machine that moves a beam of light over an object; scanners read addresses printed on packages and letters.

transport (transs-PORT)—to move or to carry something from one place to another; couriers transport packages and letters.

warehouse (WAIR-hous)—a large building used for storing or sending goods such as packages and letters

Read More

Gibson, Karen Bush. *Truck Drivers.* Community Helpers. Mankato, Minn.: Bridgestone Books, 2001.

Kottke, Jan. *A Day with a Mail Carrier.* Hard Work. New York: Children's Press, 2000.

Richardson, Adele D. *Delivery Trucks.* Transportation Library. Mankato, Minn.: Bridgestone Books, 2001.

Internet Sites

Address and Zip Code Look-Up
http://www.usps.gov/ncsc/lookups/lookups.htm
BLS Career Information
http://stats.bls.gov/k12/html/edu_over.htm

Index

bikes, 9
cars, 9
computers, 7, 13
customers, 17, 21
delivery trucks, 9
maps, 13, 17

name tags, 15
route, 13
scanners, 13
uniforms, 15
vans, 9
warehouses, 7